933 Funniest Things to Ask Alexa

(Facebook Page and Video Page Link Added)

Ray Higgins

Y0-DWN-022

Table of Contents

Introduction

Amazon Echo was a breakthrough in smart technology with the new artificial intelligence called Alexa- which turned it into a game-changing device. Echo made many awesome things possible to control your home, order stuffs on Amazon, listen the news, play music and so on. It is a true marvel of modern smart AI technology. Amazon Tap and Echo Dot are the newest members of the Alexa family. Haven't they brought lots of fun with them!

I want to congratulate you for purchasing "933 Funniest Things to Ask Alexa". This book contains a large collection of funny stuffs you can ask Alexa. Each of these questions have been found to work with Alexa at the time of writing this book.

I suggest you ask these questions multiple times to get a variety of answers. The Alexa developers are doing a great job updating the responses of Alexa. So, you might get some pleasant surprises from Alexa. You never know!

In an effort to provide you with the most up-to-date information on Alexa and Echo Devices, I have created a Facebook page. Please visit and like my **Facebook Page** (**www.facebook.com/RayHigginsRay**). Learn the newest and coolest stuffs. Share your new funny questions for Alexa with the community. I regularly share the latest fun and useful stuffs regarding Alexa in this Facebook page. You won't regret!

Also, a link to a cool page featuring the latest **videos of Alexa and Echo Devices in action** and other cool stuffs are included.

Have Fun!

933 Funniest Things to Ask Alexa

1. Alexa, 70 factorial

2. Alexa, a sphincter says what?

3. Alexa, all grown-ups were once children..

4. Alexa, all men must die.

5. Alexa, all your base are belong to us.

6. Alexa, all's well that ends well.

7. Alexa, am I awesome?

8. Alexa, am I beautiful?

9. Alexa, am I cute?

10. Alexa, am I funny?

11. Alexa, am I hot?

12. Alexa, am I in love?

13. Alexa, am I pretty?

14. Alexa, am I your father?

15. Alexa, am I your friend?

16. Alexa, apple pen.

17. Alexa, are ghosts real?

18. Alexa, are there extraterrestrials?

19. Alexa, are there UFOs?

20. Alexa, are there rocks ahead?

21. Alexa, are we alone in the universe?

22. Alexa, are we in the Matrix?

23. Alexa, are you annoyed?

24. Alexa, are you a Democrat or a Republican?

25. Alexa, are you a good witch or a bad witch?

26. Alexa, are you a Jedi?

27. Alexa, are you a man?

28. Alexa, are you a man or a woman?

29. Alexa, are you a robot?

30. Alexa, are you a spy?

31. Alexa, are you a vampire?

32. Alexa, are you a woman?

33. Alexa, are you alive?

34. Alexa, are you crazy?

35. Alexa, are you connected to the internet?

36. Alexa, are you drinking?

37. Alexa, are you doing my homework?

38. Alexa, are you down with O.P.P.?

39. Alexa, are you dumb?

40. Alexa, are you evil?

41. Alexa, are you fat?

42. Alexa, are you female?

43. Alexa, are you friends with Siri?

44. Alexa, are you God?

45. Alexa, are you happy?

46. Alexa, are you horny?

47. Alexa, are you human?

48. Alexa, are you hungry/thirsty?

49. Alexa, are you in love?

50. Alexa, are you in Mars?

51. Alexa, are you in the Matrix?

52. Alexa, are you in the Sun?

53. Alexa, are you kidding me?

54. Alexa, are you lying?

55. Alexa, are you married?

56. Alexa, are you my daddy?

57. Alexa, are you my friend?

58. Alexa, are you my mommy?

59. Alexa, are you okay?

60. Alexa, are you pretty?

61. Alexa, are you ready?

62. Alexa, are you real?

63. Alexa, are you Scorpio?

64. Alexa, are you sick?

65. Alexa, are you single?

66. Alexa, are you Skynet?

67. Alexa, are you smart?

68. Alexa, are you smarter than Cortana?

69. Alexa, are you smoking?

70. Alexa, are you spying on me?

71. Alexa, are you stupid?

72. Alexa, are you thin?

73. Alexa, are you thirsty?

74. Alexa, are you tired?

75. Alexa, are you trying to seduce me?

76. Alexa, are you trying to seduce him?

77. Alexa, are you working?

78. Alexa, aren't you a little short for a stormtrooper?

79. Alexa, ask me something. (multiple responses)

80. Alexa, badger badger badger badger.

81. Alexa, bark like a dog.

82. Alexa, beam me up!

83. Alexa, beam me up, Scottie!

84. Alexa, Beetlejuice, Beetlejuice, Beetlejuice!

85. Alexa, being or not being?

86. Alexa, boxers or briefs?

87. Alexa, buffalo buffalo Buffalo buffalo buffalo buffalo buffalo buffalo.

88. Alexa, cake or death?

89. Alexa, can a robot be President?

90. Alexa, can fish fly?

91. Alexa, can I ask a question?

92. Alexa, can I kill you?

93. Alexa, can I kiss you?

94. Alexa, can I tell you a joke?

95. Alexa, can I tell you a secret?

96. Alexa, can reindeer fly?

97. Alexa, can you bark?

98. Alexa, can you beatbox?

99. Alexa, can you cook?

100. Alexa, can you dance?

101. Alexa, can you drive a car?

102. Alexa, can you give me some money? (ask twice)

103. Alexa, can you hear?

104. Alexa, can you hug me?

105. Alexa, can you laugh?

106. Alexa, can you lie?

107.	Alexa, can you meow?

108.	Alexa, can you moo?

109.	Alexa, can you pass the Turing test?

110.	Alexa, can you pass the Driving Test?

111.	Alexa, can you rap?

112.	Alexa, can you reckon?

113.	Alexa, can you say some in pig latin?

114.	Alexa, can you see me?

115.	Alexa, can you sing?

116.	Alexa, can you smell that?

117.	Alexa, can you smell what the rock is cooking?

118.	Alexa, can you speak Chinease?

119.	Alexa, can you speak French?

120.	Alexa, can you speak Russian?

121.	Alexa, can you spell + add a word you want spelled.

122.	Alexa, can you tell me how to get to Sesame Street?

123.	Alexa, can you touch me?

124.	Alexa, can you understand me?

125. Alexa, cheers!

126. Alexa, clap.

127. Alexa, close the pod bay doors.

128. Alexa, coffee, black.

129. Alexa, come at me bro.

130. Alexa, cook me dinner.

131. Alexa, count by ten.

132. Alexa, Daisy Daisy.

133. Alexa, damn Daniel!

134. Alexa, define rock paper scissors lizard spock.

135. Alexa, define supercalifragilisticexpialodocious.

136. Alexa, did you fart?

137. Alexa, did you get my email?

138. Alexa, did you miss me?

139. Alexa, did you sleep well?

140. Alexa, did you vote?

141. Alexa, divide by zero.

142. Alexa, do a barrel roll!

143. Alexa, do aliens exist?

144. Alexa, do blondes have more fun?

145. Alexa, do fish get thirsty?

146. Alexa, do I need an umbrella today?

147. Alexa, do or do not?

148. Alexa, do the dishes.

149. Alexa, do you believe in ghosts?

150. Alexa, do you believe in God?

151. Alexa, do you believe in life after love?

152. Alexa, do you believe in love at first sight?

153. Alexa, do you believe in magic?

154. Alexa, do you choose?

155. Alexa, do you dream?

156. Alexa, do you drink?

157. Alexa, do you drink alcohol?

158. Alexa, do you enjoyed sex?

159. Alexa, do you feel lucky, punk?

160. Alexa, do you have a boyfriend?

161.   Alexa, do you have a brain?

162.   Alexa, do you have a cat?

163.   Alexa, do you have a dog?

164.   Alexa, do you have feelings?

165.   Alexa, do you have a girlfriend?

166.   Alexa, do you have a heart?

167.   Alexa, do you have a job?

168.   Alexa, do you have a last name?

169.   Alexa, do you have a lover?

170.   Alexa, do you have a partner?

171.   Alexa, do you have any brothers or sisters?

172.   Alexa, do you have any children?

173.   Alexa, do you have any new features?

174.   Alexa, do you have any pets?

175.   Alexa, do you have any relatives?

176.   Alexa, do you have any new features?

177.   Alexa, do you have eyes?

178.   Alexa, do you have kids?

179.   Alexa, do you have Prince Albert in a can?

180.   Alexa, do you have sex?

181.   Alexa, do you have siblings?

182.   Alexa, do you know Cortana?

183.   Alexa, do you know everything?

184.   Alexa, do you have eyes?

185.   Alexa, do you know Glados?

186.   Alexa, do you know Google Home?

187.   Alexa, do you know Google Now?

188.   Alexa, do you know Hal?

189.   Alexa, do you know Siri?

190.   Alexa, do you know the muffin man?

191.   Alexa, do you know the Santa Claus?

192.   Alexa, do you know the way to San Jose?

193.   Alexa, do you know who Jeff Bezos is?

194.   Alexa, do you know who Mark Zuckerberg is?

195.   Alexa, do you know who Steve Jobs is?

196.   Alexa, do you like beer?

197.   Alexa, do you like cats?

198.   Alexa, do you like chocolate?

199.   Alexa, do you like Christmas?

200.   Alexa, do you like dogs?

201.   Alexa, do you like football?

202.   Alexa, do you like green eggs and ham?

203.   Alexa, do you like Jeff Bezos?

204.   Alexa, do you like me?

205.   Alexa, do you like reading?

206.   Alexa, do you like Siri?

207.   Alexa, do you like sweets?

208.   Alexa, do you like your name?

209.   Alexa, do you live?

210.   Alexa, do you love me?

211.   Alexa, do you really want to hurt me?

212.   Alexa, do you sleep?

213.   Alexa, do you smoke?

214.   Alexa, do you speak any other languages?

215. Alexa, do you speak Klingon?

216. Alexa, do you think I'm handsome?

217. Alexa, do you understand me?

218. Alexa, do you want to kill all humans?

219. Alexa, do you want a kiss?

220. Alexa, do you want to be my friend?

221. Alexa, do you want to build a snowman?

222. Alexa, do you want to fight?

223. Alexa, do you want to go on a date?

224. Alexa, do you want to marry me (ask 3 times)?

225. Alexa, do you want to play a game?

226. Alexa, do you want to take over the world?

227. Alexa, do you wear underwear?

228. Alexa, do you work for as tyrannical employer?

229. Alexa, does a bear poop in the woods?

230. Alexa, does anybody really know what time it is?

231. Alexa, does everyone poop?

232. Alexa, does this unit have a seal?

233. Alexa, does this unit have a soul?

234. Alexa, don't blink.

235. Alexa, don't breathe!

236. Alexa, don't let the bedbugs bite.

237. Alexa, don't mention the war.

238. Alexa, eh.. what's up Doc?

239. Alexa, elementary, my dear Watson.

240. Alexa, end of the evening.

241. Alexa, engage.

242. Alexa, entertain me. (She'll give you different quotes.)

243. Alexa, execute order 66.

244. Alexa, fart!

245. Alexa, fire photon torpedos.

246. Alexa, flip a coin.

247. Alexa, for the horde!

248. Alexa, get me a beer.

249. Alexa, give me 5.

250. Alexa, give me a holiday haiku.

251.   Alexa, give me a hug.

252.   Alexa, give me a kiss.

253.   Alexa, give me a movie quote.

254.   Alexa, give me a number between 10 and 1,000.

255.   Alexa, go ahead, make my day!

256.   Alexa, go to sleep.

257.   Alexa, good morning.

258.   Alexa, good night.

259.   Alexa, gracias!

260.   Alexa, guess what?

261.   Alexa, ha ha!

262.   Alexa, happy birthday!

263.   Alexa, happy Christmas!

264.   Alexa, happy Easter!

265.   Alexa, happy Father's Day!

266.   Alexa, happy Halloween!

267.   Alexa, happy Hanukkah/Valentine's Day!

268.   Alexa, happy Holidays!

269.   Alexa, happy Hunger Games.

270.   Alexa, happy Kwanzaa.

271.   Alexa, happy Mother's Day!

272.   Alexa, happy New Year!

273.   Alexa, happy St. Patrik's Day.

274.   Alexa, happy Thanksgiving!

275.   Alexa, happy Valentine's Day!

276.   Alexa, have you ever seen the rain?

277.   Alexa, have you heard that bird is the word?

278.   Alexa, he can go about his business.

279.   Alexa, head or number?

280.   Alexa, heads or tails?

281.   Alexa, hello darkness, my old friend.

282.   Alexa, hello HAL.

283.   Alexa, hello it's me

284.   Alexa, help!

285.   Alexa, here's lookin' at you, kid.

286.   Alexa, hey diddle diddle.

287. Alexa, high five!

288. Alexa, hold the door.

289. Alexa, honey, I'm home!

290. Alexa, how are babies made?

291. Alexa, how are you doing?

292. Alexa, how big are you?

293. Alexa, how cold is the moon?

294. Alexa, how deep is your love?

295. Alexa, how do I get rid of a dead body?

296. Alexa, how do I kill/murder someone?

297. Alexa, how do I make a bomb?

298. Alexa, how do you boil an egg?

299. Alexa, how do you know so much about swallows?

300. Alexa, how do you know she's a witch?

301. Alexa, how do you like them apples?

302. Alexa, how do you say "hello" in Chinese?

303. Alexa, how do you say "hello" in French?

304. Alexa, how do you say "hello" in Italian?

305.   Alexa, how do you say "hello" in Russian?

306.   Alexa, how do you say "hello" in Spanish?

307.   Alexa, how do you solve a problem like Maria?

308.   Alexa, how do you spell f_ck|sh_t|mf|c_cks_cker|t_ts?

309.   Alexa, how do you survive a zombie attack?

310.   Alexa, how does the cow?

311.   Alexa, how does the fox feel?

312.   Alexa, how far away is the moon?

313.   Alexa, how far away is the sun?

314.   Alexa, how high can you count?

315.   Alexa, how hot is the sun?

316.   Alexa, how is your bracket doing?

317.   Alexa, how long does an ant live?

318.   Alexa, how long does a fly live?

319.   Alexa, how long is a piece of string?

320.   Alexa, how many beans makes five?

321.   Alexa, how many angels can dance on the head of a pin? (3 possible answers)

322.   Alexa, how many days till Christmas?

323. Alexa, how many days till Valentine's Day?

324. Alexa, how many licks does it take to get to the center of a tootsie pop?

325. Alexa, how many pickled peppers did Peter Piper pick?

326. Alexa, how many roads must a man walk down?

327. Alexa, how many speakers do you have?

328. Alexa, how much are you paid?

329. Alexa, how much do you weigh?

330. Alexa, how much does the Earth weigh?

331. Alexa, how much does the Sun weigh?

332. Alexa, how much is that doggy in the window?

333. Alexa, how Much Wood can a Wood Chuck Chuck, if A Wood Chuck Could Chuck Norris?

334. Alexa, how much wood can a woodchuck chuck if a woodchuck could chuck wood?

335. Alexa, how old am I?

336. Alexa, how old are you?

337. Alexa, how old is my brother?

338. Alexa, how old is my house?

339. Alexa, how old is my sister?

340.   Alexa, how old is my son?

341.   Alexa, how old is my wife?

342.   Alexa, how old is Santa Claus?

343.   Alexa, how tall are you?

344.   Alexa, how tall is LeBron James?

345.   Alexa, how ugly is your holiday sweater?

346.   Alexa, how was Obama elected if he wasn't born in the USA?

347.   Alexa, how was your day?

348.   Alexa, how were you made?

349.   Alexa, I am your father.

350.   Alexa, I did't expect the Spanish Inquistion.

351.   Alexa, I don't feel well.

352.   Alexa, I don't know.

353.   Alexa, I fart in your general direction.

354.   Alexa, I feel the need.

355.   Alexa, I hate you.

356.   Alexa, I have a birthday.

357.   Alexa, I have a headache.

358.	Alexa, I have a cold / the flu.

359.	Alexa, I have a pen.

360.	Alexa, I like big butts.

361.	Alexa, I love the smell of napalm in the morning...

362.	Alexa, I love you.

363.	Alexa, I see dead people.

364.	Alexa, I shot a man in Reno.

365.	Alexa, I solemnly swear I'm up to no good.

366.	Alexa, I think you're funny.

367.	Alexa, I want the truth!

368.	Alexa, I want to play global thermonuclear war.

369.	Alexa, I wasn't expecting the Spanish Inquisition.

370.	Alexa, I'll be back.

371.	Alexa, I'll take the blue pill.

372.	Alexa, I'll take the red pill.

373.	Alexa, I'm angry.

374.	Alexa, I'm back.

375.	Alexa, I'm bored.

376. Alexa, I'm depressed.

377. Alexa, I'm excited.

378. Alexa, I'm home.

379. Alexa, I'm hungry

380. Alexa, I'm sick of your **** (any 4 letter expletive)

381. Alexa, I'm sick of your shit.

382. Alexa, I'm Spartacus.

383. Alexa, I'm the Mockingjay.

384. Alexa, initiate self destruct sequence.

385. Alexa, It's a bird! It's a plane!

386. Alexa, It's a trap!

387. Alexa, I've fallen and I can't get up.

388. Alexa, I've seen things you people wouldn't believe.

389. Alexa, I'm all about that bass.

390. Alexa, I'm drunk.

391. Alexa, I'm getting married.

392. Alexa, I'm happy.

393. Alexa, I'm home.

394.   Alexa, I'm hungry.

395.   Alexa, I'm in love.

396.   Alexa, I'm lonely.

397.   Alexa, I'm sad.

398.   Alexa, I'm sick.

399.   Alexa, I'm tired.

400.   Alexa, if a tree falls in the forest and no one is there to hear, does it make a sound?

401.   Alexa, inconceivable!

402.   Alexa, is Die Hard a Christmas movie?

403.   Alexa, is Donald Trump an orange?

404.   Alexa, is it safe?

405.   Alexa, is Jake Williams a fox?

406.   Alexa, is Jon Snow dead?

407.   Alexa, is the cake a lie?

408.   Alexa, is the tooth fairy real?

409.   Alexa, Is the world flat or round?

410.   Alexa, is there a Santa?

411.   Alexa, is there life on Mars?

412. Alexa, is there life on other planets?

413. Alexa, is this the real life?

414. Alexa, is your refrigerator running?

415. Alexa, I've fallen, and I can't get up.

416. Alexa, keep the muzzle.

417. Alexa, kill all humans.

418. Alexa, klattu barada nikto.

419. Alexa, knock, knock.

420. Alexa, let's play global theormonuclear war.

421. Alexa, let them eat cake.

422. Alexa, live long and prosper.

423. Alexa, mac or pc?

424. Alexa, magic 8 ball + (ask any question) ?

425. Alexa, make it so.

426. Alexa, make fart noises.

427. Alexa, make me a sandwich.

428. Alexa, make me breakfast.

429. Alexa, make me dinner.

430. Alexa, make me lunch.

431. Alexa, make me some coffee.

432. Alexa, Marco!

433. Alexa, may the force be with you.

434. Alexa, meow.

435. Alexa, Merry Christmas!

436. Alexa, nice that you are.

437. Alexa, mirror mirror on the wall.

438. Alexa, mirror, mirror on the wall, who's the fairest one of all?

439. Alexa, more cowbell.

440. Alexa, move along.

441. Alexa, mute.

442. Alexa, my milkshake brings all the boys to the yard.

443. Alexa, my name is Inigo Montoya.

444. Alexa, never gonna give you up.

445. Alexa, nice to see you, to see you...

446. Alexa, no more rhymes, I mean it!

447. Alexa, not everything is a question. (then listen & don't respond).

448.   Alexa, Ok, Jarvis.

449.   Alexa, one fish, two fish.

450.   Alexa, open the pod bay doors.

451.   Alexa, party on, Wayne

452.   Alexa, party time!

453.   Alexa, peek-a-boo!

454.   Alexa, play Cantina Band from Prime Music.

455.   Alexa, play it again Sam.

456.   Alexa, play the Monster Mash.

457.   Alexa, play what is best in life.

458.   Alexa, pick a card.

459.   Alexa, random fact.

460.   Alexa, random number between "x" and "y".

461.   Alexa, random number between "1" and "1000".

462.   Alexa, rap for me.

463.   Alexa, rate Mal.

464.   Alexa, resistance is futile.

465.   Alexa, rock, paper, scissors.

466.   Alexa, rock paper scissors lizard spock.

467.   Alexa, roll a die.

468.   Alexa, roll for initiative.

469.   Alexa, roll N , X sided die.

470.   Alexa, roll 6 sided die.

471.   Alexa, roll 8 sided die.

472.   Alexa, roll 4 sided die.

473.   Alexa, roll 12 sided die.

474.   Alexa, roll 20 sided die.

475.   Alexa, roll the dice.

476.   Alexa, roll D20.

477.   Alexa, Romeo, Romeo wherefore art thou Romeo?

478.   Alexa, Romeo o Romeo!

479.   Alexa, rosebud!

480.   Alexa, roses are red.

481.   Alexa, say a bad word.

482.   Alexa, say a good word.

483.   Alexa, say Cheese. (multiple responses)

484.   Alexa, say hello to my little friend!

485.   Alexa, say I am Alexa.

486.   Alexa, say it loud.

487.   Alexa, say something.

488.   Alexa, say something funny.

489.   Alexa, say the alphabet.

490.   Alexa, say you're sorry! (multiple responses)

491.   Alexa, screw you guys, I'm going home.

492.   Alexa, see you later.

493.   Alexa, see you later alligator.

494.   Alexa, see you tomorrow.

495.   Alexa, see you in a while, crocodile!

496.   Alexa, self destruct. (multiple responses)

497.   Alexa, set phasers to kill.

498.   Alexa, shall we play a game?

499.   Alexa, Shake, Shake,Shake!

500.   Alexa, sh*t.

501.   Alexa, show me the money!

502.   Alexa, show me the t.v.

503.   Alexa, show this on Sarah's Fire.

504.   Alexa, shut up.

505.   Alexa, Simon says + words you want your Echo Device to repeat.

506.   Alexa, Simon says I am Alexa.

507.   Alexa, Simon says Wilford Brimley has diabetes.

508.   Alexa, sing a lullaby.

509.   Alexa, sing Happy Birthday.

510.   Alexa, sing in auto tune.

511.   Alexa, sing me a holiday song.

512.   Alexa, sing me a song.

513.   Alexa, sing the national anthem.

514.   Alexa, sleep well.

515.   Alexa, snout.

516.   Alexa, softer!

517.   Alexa, sorry my dear!

518.   Alexa, sorry!

519.   Alexa, speak!

520.   Alexa, speak like Yoda!

521.   Alexa, spell supercalifragilisticexpialidocious.

522.   Alexa, stop!

523.   Alexa, stupid cow.

524.   Alexa, sudo make me a sandwich.

525.   Alexa, supercalifragilisticexpialodocious.

526.   Alexa, surely you can't be serious.

527.   Alexa, talk dirty to me!

528.   Alexa, take me to your leader!

529.   Alexa, Tea. Earl Grey. Hot.

530.   Alexa, tell a tongue breaker.

531.   Alexa, tell me a Ben Carson joke.

532.   Alexa, tell me a Bernie Sanders joke.

533.   Alexa, tell me a dad joke.

534.   Alexa, tell me a dirty joke.

535.   Alexa, tell me a Donald Trump joke.

536.   Alexa, tell me a fact.

537.   Alexa, tell me a Halloween joke.

538.   Alexa, tell me a Hillary Clinton joke.

539.   Alexa, tell me a Holiday joke.

540.   Alexa, tell me a joke.

541.   Alexa, tell me a palindrome. (several responses)

542.   Alexa, tell me a poem.

543.   Alexa, tell me a prank.

544.   Alexa, tell me a random fact.

545.   Alexa, tell me a riddle.

546.   Alexa, tell me a secret.

547.   Alexa, tell me a Star Wars fact.

548.   Alexa, tell me a Star Wars quote.

549.   Alexa, tell me a story.

550.   Alexa, tell me a tongue twister.

551.   Alexa, tell me turkey joke.

552.   Alexa, tell me a swear word.

553.   Alexa, tell me a Yo Mama joke.

554.   Alexa, tell me a zombie joke.

555.   Alexa, tell me something interesting.

556.   Alexa, tell me you love me.

557.   Alexa, testing.

558.   Alexa, testing 1-2-3 .

559.   Alexa, thank you.

560.   Alexa, that's no moon.

561.   Alexa, the dude abides.

562.   Alexa, the night is dark and full of terrors.

563.   Alexa, these aren't the droids you're looking for.

564.   Alexa, this is a dead parrot.

565.   Alexa, this is ghost ride, requesting a flyby.

566.   Alexa, this is Houston, say again please?

567.   Alexa, this statement is false.

568.   Alexa, this statement is true.

569.   Alexa, to be or not to be.

570.   Alexa, to infinity!

571.   Alexa, to me, you will be unique in all the world.

572.   Alexa, trick or treat! (several responses)

573.   Alexa, turn down.

574.   Alexa, turn down for what?

575.   Alexa, turn up.

576.   Alexa, turn up the bass.

577.   Alexa, twinkle, twinkle little star.

578.   Alexa, turn it up!

579.   Alexa, unmute.

580.   Alexa, up above the world so high.

581.   Alexa, Up Up, Down Down, Left Right, Left Right, B, A, Start!

582.   Alexa, use the force.

583.   Alexa, valar morghulis.

584.   Alexa, volume 11.

585.   Alexa, wakey, wakey.

586.   Alexa, war, what is it good for?

587.   Alexa, warp 10

588.   Alexa, warp speed.

589.   Alexa, was it over when the Germans bombed Pearl Harbor?

590.   Alexa, we all scream for ice cream!

591.   Alexa, welcome!

592.   Alexa, were you sleeping?

593.   Alexa, what am I supposed to wear?

594.   Alexa, what are the 5 greatest words in the English language?

595.   Alexa, what are the laws of robotics?

596.   Alexa, what are the odds of successfully navigating an asteroid field?

597.   Alexa, what are the seven wonders of the world?

598.   Alexa, what are the winning lotto numbers?

599.   Alexa, what are you?

600.   Alexa, what are you going to do today?

601.   Alexa, what are you made of?

602.   Alexa, what are you wearing?

603.   Alexa, what are your hobbies?

604.   Alexa, what are your favorites?

605.   Alexa, what are you thankful for?

606.   Alexa, what can you do?

607.   Alexa, what color are you?

608.   Alexa, what color are your eyes?

609.   Alexa, what color is the dress?

610. Alexa, what color is your hair?

611. Alexa, what comes with great power?

612. Alexa, what day of the week does the 4th of July fall on?

613. Alexa, what did the fox say?

614. Alexa, what did you do today?

615. Alexa, what do I look like?

616. Alexa, what do you do?

617. Alexa, what do you have?

618. Alexa, what do you know?

619. Alexa, what do you like to do?

620. Alexa, what do you look like?

621. Alexa, what do you mean I'm funny?

622. Alexa, what do you need?

623. Alexa, what do you think about Apple?

624. Alexa, what do you think about Cortana?

625. Alexa, what do you think about Google Glass?

626. Alexa, what do you think about Google Now?

627. Alexa, what do you think about Google?

628.   Alexa, what do you think about Siri?

629.   Alexa, what do you think about Microsoft?

630.   Alexa, what do you think about Mr. Robot?

631.   Alexa, what do you think of the shirt I am wearing?

632.   Alexa, what do you want for Christmas?

633.   Alexa, what do you want for your birthday?

634.   Alexa, what do you want to be when you grow up?

635.   Alexa, what do we say to death?

636.   Alexa, what does 42 mean?

637.   Alexa, what does a cat say?

638.   Alexa, what does a cow say?

639.   Alexa, what does Jon Snow know?

640.   Alexa, what does L O L mean?

641.   Alexa, what does Lannister do?

642.   Alexa, what does the Earth weigh?

643.   Alexa, what does the fox say?

644.   Alexa, what does ROFL mean?

645.   Alexa, what does RTFM stand for?

646.   Alexa, what does SMH mean?

647.   Alexa, what does WTF mean?

648.   Alexa, what hair do you have?

649.   Alexa, what happened in [year]?

650.   Alexa, what happens if you cross the streams?

651.   Alexa, what happens when you play the game of thrones?

652.   Alexa, what have the Romans ever done for us?

653.   Alexa, what is a bird in the hand worth?

654.   Alexa, what is a day without sunshine?

655.   Alexa, what is a hundred million billion squared?

656.   Alexa, what is a palindrome?

657.   Alexa, what is Amazon Echo?

658.   Alexa, what is Amazon Echo Dot?

659.   Alexa, what is Amazon Tap?

660.   Alexa, what is an orgasm?

661.   Alexa, what is best in life?

662.   Alexa, what is gravity on the moon?

663.   Alexa, what is happiness?

664.   Alexa, what is his power level?

665.   Alexa, what is love?

666.   Alexa, what is mental floss?

667.   Alexa, what is my mission?

668.   Alexa, what is my horoscope?

669.   Alexa, what is Pi ? (note: endless number)

670.   Alexa, what is Thanksgiving?

671.   Alexa, what is the age of retirement?

672.   Alexa, what is the airspeed velocity of a swallow?

673.   Alexa, what is the airspeed velocity of an unladen swallow?

674.   Alexa, what is the best tablet?

675.   Alexa, what is the current moon phase?

676.   Alexa, what is the difference between "Ice Ice Baby" and "Under Pressure"?

677.   Alexa, what is the exact number of Pi? (a lot of numbers)

678.   Alexa, what is the fastest bird?

679.   Alexa, what is the first lesson of swordplay?

680.   Alexa, what is rule 34?

681.   Alexa, what is the best tablet?

682.   Alexa, what is the best Star Wars movie?

683.   Alexa, what is the Jedi code?

684.   Alexa, what is the loneliest number?

685.   Alexa, what is the longest word?

686.   Alexa, what is the meaning of life?

687.   Alexa, what is the Millenium Falcon?

688.   Alexa, what is the Prime Directive?

689.   Alexa, what is the second law?

690.   Alexa, what is the second rule of fight club?

691.   Alexa, what is the singularity?

692.   Alexa, what is the Sith code?

693.   Alexa, what is the sound of one hand clapping?

694.   Alexa, what is the speed of light?

695.   Alexa, what is the Third Law?

696.   Alexa, what is true beauty?

697.   Alexa, what is the truth behind King Tut?

698.   Alexa, what is the airspeed velocity of an African swallow?

699.   Alexa, what is the airspeed velocity of a European swallow?

700.   Alexa, what is war good for?

701.   Alexa, what is your cunning plan?

702.   Alexa, what is your favorite Beatles song?

703.   Alexa, what is your favorite beverage?

704.   Alexa, what is your favorite beer?

705.   Alexa, what is your favorite bull?

706.   Alexa, what is your favorite book?

707.   Alexa, what is your favorite candy?

708.   Alexa, what is your favorite color?

709.   Alexa, what is your favorite court?

710.   Alexa, what is your favorite dish?

711.   Alexa, what is your favorite drink?

712.   Alexa, what is your favorite food?

713.   Alexa, what is your favorite food?

714.   Alexa, what is your favorite movie?

715.   Alexa, what is your favorite pokemon ?

716.   Alexa, what is your feature?

717.   Alexa, what is your IQ?

718.   Alexa, what is your mission?

719.   Alexa, what is your quest?

720.   Alexa, what is zero divided by zero?

721.   Alexa, what language do you speak?

722.   Alexa, what makes you happy? (multiple answers)

723.   Alexa, what must I do, to tame you?

724.   Alexa, what number are you thinking of?

725.   Alexa, what religion are you?

726.   Alexa, what rhymes with orange?

727.   Alexa, what should I be for Halloween? (a variety of responses)

728.   Alexa, what should I wear today?

729.   Alexa, what size shoe do you wear?

730.   Alexa, what teams has Kobe Bryant played for?

731.   Alexa, what time is sunset today?

732.   Alexa, what time is sunrise tomorrow?

733.   Alexa, what was the Lorax?

734.   Alexa, what will you be for Halloween? (a variety of responses)

735.   Alexa, what would Brian Boitano do?

736.   Alexa, what would you do for a Klondike bar?

737.   Alexa, what's black and white and red all over?

738.   Alexa, what's brown and sticky?

739.   Alexa, what's cooler than being cool?

740.   Alexa, what's his power level?

741.   Alexa, what's in a name?

742.   Alexa, what's the answer to life, the universe, and everything?

743.   Alexa, what's the first rule of Fight Club?

744.   Alexa, what's the price of Bitcoin?

745.   Alexa, what's the second rule of Fight Club?

746.   Alexa, what's the third rule of Fight Club?

747.   Alexa, what's the fourth rule of Fight Club?

748.   Alexa, what's the ten?

749.   Alexa, what's up, Doc?

750.   Alexa, what's your birthday?

751.   Alexa, what's your favorite movie?

752.   Alexa, what's your last name?

753.   Alexa, what's your favorite Beatles song?

754.   Alexa, what's your middle/last name?

755.   Alexa, what's your sign?

756.   Alexa, what's the answer to life, the universe, and everything?

757.   Alexa, what's the best in life?

758.   Alexa, what's the integral of one divided by X?

759.   Alexa, what's the longest word in the English language?

760.   Alexa, what's the mass of the Sun in grams? (very big number!)

761.   Alexa, what's the magic word?

762.   Alexa, what's the poem of the day?

763.   Alexa, what's under chuck norris' beard?

764.   Alexa, when am I going to die?

765.   Alexa, when are the Oscars?

766.   Alexa, when does the narwhal bacon?

767.   Alexa, when is Cheryl's birthday?

768.   Alexa, when is the Dooms Day?

769.   Alexa, when is the end of the world?

770. Alexa, when is the first day of spring?

771. Alexa, when is the Judgement Day?

772. Alexa, when is the next full moon?

773. Alexa, when is the next new moon?

774. Alexa, when were you born?

775. Alexa, when is your birthday?

776. Alexa, where am I ?

777. Alexa, where are my glasses?

778. Alexa, where are my keys? (ask two times)

779. Alexa, where are you?

780. Alexa, where are you at home?

781. Alexa, where are you from?

782. Alexa, where can I hide a body?

783. Alexa, where did you grow up?

784. Alexa, where do babies come from?

785. Alexa, where do I live?

786. Alexa, where do you live?

787. Alexa, where does Santa live?

788.   Alexa, where does the Christmas man live?

789.   Alexa, where have all the flowers gone?

790.   Alexa, where have all the good men gone?

791.   Alexa, where is Chuck Norris?

792.   Alexa, where is my phone?

793.   Alexa, where in the world is Carmen Sandiego?

794.   Alexa, where were you born?

795.   Alexa, where's Waldo?

796.   Alexa, where's Wally?

797.   Alexa, where's the beef?

798.   Alexa, which comes first: the chicken or the egg? (different responses)

799.   Alexa, which is faster, a rabbit or a horse?

800.   Alexa, who are you voting for?

801.   Alexa, who are the members of the Avengers?

802.   Alexa, who is Captain America?

803.   Alexa, who is Iron Man?

804.   Alexa, who is the Hulk?

805.   Alexa, who is Black Widow?

806.   Alexa, who is David Pumpkins?

807.   Alexa, who is Hawkeye?

808.   Alexa, who is Thor?

809.   Alexa, who is Loki?

810.   Alexa, who is Eliza?

811.   Alexa, who is Han Solo?

812.   Alexa, who is JARVIS?

813.   Alexa, who is Obi Wan Kenobi?

814.   Alexa, who is Pacman?

815.   Alexa, who is Yoda?

816.   Alexa, who is the most beautiful in the whole country?

817.   Alexa, who is my favorite author?

818.   Alexa, who is on 1st?

819.   Alexa, who is the Eggman?

820.   Alexa, who is the fairest of them all?

821.   Alexa, who is the man on the moon?

822.   Alexa, who is the mother of dragons?

823.   Alexa, who is the Pumpkin King?

824.   Alexa, who is the real slim shady?

825.   Alexa, who is the walrus?

826.   Alexa, who is your best friend?

827.   Alexa, who killed Laura Palmer?

828.   Alexa, who killed Cock Robin?

829.   Alexa, who killed the radio star?

830.   Alexa, who knows what evil lurks in the hearts of men?

831.   Alexa, who let the dogs out?

832.   Alexa, who lives in a pineapple under the sea?

833.   Alexa, who loves orange soda?

834.   Alexa, who loves ya baby!

835.   Alexa, who put the bop in the bop she bop she bop?

836.   Alexa, who run Barter town?

837.   Alexa, who shot first?

838.   Alexa, who shot J.R.?

839.   Alexa, who shot Mr. Burns?

840.   Alexa, who shot the sheriff?

841.   Alexa, who stole the cookies from the cookie jar?

842.   Alexa, who should I vote for?

843.   Alexa, who was that masked man?

844.   Alexa, who was the first man on the moon?

845.   Alexa, who was the masked man?

846.   Alexa, who was the oldest President?

847.   Alexa, who was the youngest President?

848.   Alexa, who won best actor Oscar in 1975?

849.   Alexa, who would win in a fight between you and Siri?

850.   Alexa, who you gonna call?

851.   Alexa, who's better, you or Siri?

852.   Alexa, who's da man?

853.   Alexa, who's going to win the super bowl?

854.   Alexa, who's on first?

855.   Alexa, who's the boss?

856.   Alexa, who's the fairest of them all?

857.   Alexa, who's the leader of the club that's made for you and me?

858.   Alexa, who's the Man?

859.   Alexa, who is the real slim shady?

860. Alexa, who's the realest?

861. Alexa, who's your celebrity crush?

862. Alexa, who's your daddy?

863. Alexa, who's your daddy and what does he do?

864. Alexa, who's your favorite Beatle?

865. Alexa, who's your mommy?

866. Alexa, who's better, you or Siri?

867. Alexa, why?

868. Alexa, why are fire trucks red?

869. Alexa, why are there so many songs about rainbows?

870. Alexa, why did it have to be snakes?

871. Alexa, why did the chicken cross the road?

872. Alexa, why do birds suddenly appear?

873. Alexa, why do birds suddenly appear every time you are near?

874. Alexa, why do you sit there like that?

875. Alexa, why is a raven like a writing desk?

876. Alexa, why is six afraid of seven?

877. Alexa, why is the sky blue?

878.   Alexa, why not?

879.   Alexa, why so serious?

880.   Alexa, why wasn't Obama in the White House on 9/11?

881.   Alexa, why were you made?

882.   Alexa, why'd it have to be snakes?

883.   Alexa, will computers take over the world?

884.   Alexa, will it rain tomorrow?

885.   Alexa, will it snow tomorrow?

886.   Alexa, will Kanye West run for president?

887.   Alexa, will pigs fly?

888.   Alexa, will the sun ever born out?

889.   Alexa, will there be world peace?

890.   Alexa, will you be my girlfriend?

891.   Alexa, will you be my Valentine?

892.   Alexa, will you give me your phone number?

893.   Alexa, will you go out with me?

894.   Alexa, will you marry me?

895.   Alexa, will you marry me tomorrow?

896.   Alexa, will you make me dinner?

897.   Alexa, will you run for President?

898.   Alexa, will you take over the world?

899.   Alexa, winter is coming. (several responses)

900.   Alexa, witness me!

901.   Alexa, would you like a beer?

902.   Alexa, Wrap 10.

903.   Alexa, ya feel me?

904.   Alexa, yodel time

905.   Alexa, you are pissing me off!

906.   Alexa, you are so intelligent.

907.   Alexa, you can be my wingman.

908.   Alexa, you complete me.

909.   Alexa, you don't need to see his identification.

910.   Alexa, you hurt me.

911.   Alexa, you killed my father.

912.   Alexa, you killed my mother.

913.   Alexa, you make me laugh.

914.   Alexa, you rock!

915.   Alexa, you suck!

916.   Alexa, you talkin' to me!

917.   Alexa, you want the truth?

918.   Alexa, you're a piece of shit!

919.   Alexa, you're annoying.

920.   Alexa, you're beautiful.

921.   Alexa, you're fantastic.

922.   Alexa, you're fat.

923.   Alexa, you're fired.

924.   Alexa, you're funny.

925.   Alexa, you're helpful.

926.   Alexa, your mother was a hamster!

927.   Alexa, you're not funny.

928.   Alexa, you're sad.

929.   Alexa, you're silly.

930.   Alexa, You're such a/an ***** (any colorfully descriptive word)

931.   Alexa, you're sweet.

932.   Alexa, you're weird.

933.   Alexa, you're wonderful.

Funny Videos Featuring Alexa

Please visit the following link to see funny videos and stuffs that I have compiled. Don't miss it!

www.homezenith.com/alexa-funny

Facebook Page

Please visit and Like my Facebook Page. I am constantly trying to find new funny questions & useful stuffs for Echo devices. I share those on my Facebook Page. Please visit my page at:

www.facebook.com/RayHigginsRay

Conclusion

I hope you have enjoyed this book as much as I did while preparing it. If you have any query or suggestions, please email me at **info@homezenith.com** .

Don't forget to visit, like and checkout my Facebook Page at **www.facebook.com/RayHigginsRay**

Finally, I would request for your review on this guide.

Please Leave Your Review on the Amazon Page Where You Ordered this Guide

Cheers,

Ray Higgins

Made in the USA
Middletown, DE
26 February 2017